DAVID HOPKINS

CONTENTS

Dear Real Food Rocker,

For those of us involved with the Public Health Collaboration (PHC) we are big fans of the real food lifestyle. We are also interested in being at our best and helping those we work with to achieve their highest possible well-being. We have all discovered over the years how much better we feel eating real food and are convinced by the science underpinning this lifestyle. Have a look on the PHC website for our FREE real food booklets about how you can follow a real food lifestyle for health and for weight loss as well as lots of other free resources @ www.PublicHealthCollaboration.org

We are asked on a regular basis questions such as "so what do you eat?", "what about packed lunches?", "what if I want to feed the whole family?" or "how do you cope eating out?". This book is a collection of our favourite, easy to prepare real food recipes from some of our board of doctors and our public members from around the world.

As this book is a collaboration between lots of real food rockers it isn't as formal or professionally photographed as most cook books, but hopefully because it comes from normal people who are strapped for time it gives it some genuine charm. With that in mind, we cannot take any responsibility if anything goes wrong with any of the recipes.

Finally, be sure to send us photos of your creations from this cook book on Twitter @PHCukorg or our Facebook page, www.facebook.com/PHCukorg , with the hashtag #RealFoodRocks

ROCK ON REAL FOOD ROCKERS :) TEAM PHC

Dr. Jen Unwin – Clinical Psychologist – Twitter @jen_unwin

Dr. Jen Unwin has worked in the NHS for nearly 30 years and over this time has been interested in how it is that people can cope and even thrive with long-term health challenges. She believes that patients who are able to maintain their hopefulness and emotional well-being in the face of illness have better quality of life, experience fewer symptoms, take less medication, consult less and even live longer. Dr. Unwin is the chair of the UK Association for Solution Focused Practice.

Dr. Joanne McCormack – General Practitioner – Twitter @JoanneReynold14

Dr. McCormack has been a GP for 24 years and was a GP partner in Warrington up until April 2015. She was also a GP Trainer, and now works as a sessional GP in two training practices as well as the Named GP for Safeguarding Children for an area of 300,000 people. Over the past 30 years that she has been a doctor she has seen the incidence of diabetes go up five fold in her town, something that has been echoed nationally.

Dr. Trudi Deakin – Dietitian – Twitter @XPERTHealth

Trudi is Chief Executive of the registered charity X-PERT Health, which specialises in the research, development, implementation and audit of structured education for the public and healthcare professionals. Trudi's first degree in 1993 was Nutrition and Dietetics, followed by a teaching qualification in 1998 and a doctorate in diabetes in 2004.

Dr. David Unwin – General Practitioner – Twitter @LowCarbGP

A GP based in Southport, Dr. Unwin is the RCGP National Champion for Collaborative Care and Support Planning in Obesity & Diabetes, as well as a Clinical Expert in diabetes. In 2016 he won the NHS Innovator of the Year Award. He has published his work in Practical Diabetes, Diabesity in Practice and in the BMJ.

Samuel Feltham – Director, Public Health Collaboration – Twitter @SamFeltham

Samuel has been in the health and fitness industry for over a decade. Starting out at a sports centre and working his way up to studying at the European Institute of Fitness as a Master Personal Trainer. After 5 years of running a fitness boot camp he decided to move on, in order to fully focus on the Public Health Collaboration.

Once you start a real food lifestyle your shopping habits change quite a bit. With that in mind, it's a good idea to always have these ingredients in your cupboard or fridge as you will see them in many of the recipe ideas contained in this cook book. Try to buy the best quality your budget will stretch to (grass fed, free range, organic) and if you have time, be sure to buy local!

- Olive oil (buy it in larger quantities to get it cheaper)
- Coconut oil (great for curries and "cakes")
- Butter (grass-fed e.g., Kerrygold) *Anchor, Lurpak*
- Greek yoghurt
- Cream
- Eggs
- Cheese
- Spices and herbs
- Mustard (no added sugar)
- Red onions
- Peppers
- Mushrooms
- Tomatoes
- Lots of green vegetables (green beans, leeks, courgettes, broccoli, spinach, cabbage etc.)
- Fruit (avocado, tomato, blueberries, raspberries, strawberries)
- Meat (chicken, beef, lamb, pork etc.)
- Fish
- Seeds and nuts
- Ground almonds
- Tinned tomatoes, puréed tomatoes or passata

Most main meals are made up of a nice piece of protein (meat or fish), a pile of vegetables or salad and some kind of tasty sauce or flavour combination.

BREAKFASTS

It is always good to have a range of breakfast options for at home, the office and travelling, so hopefully the following recipes will give you some good ideas which you can adapt to your own taste.

Katie has been a member of Dr David Unwin's low-carb group in Southport for many years now and she ALWAYS has this for breakfast! You can make an individual one in a small pot or multiply up for more people. It can be microwaved or baked. You can adapt it to be 'sweet' or 'savoury' and so can use it for lunches too.

INGREDIENTS (1 MUFFIN):

- 1 egg
- Knob of melted butter or 2 tsp coconut or olive oil
- 1/4 cup of ground almonds (50g)
- Half a grated apple or pear (optional)
- Vanilla powder/cocoa powder/cinnamon/mixed spice as per your taste
- 1/2 tsp baking powder

DIRECTIONS:

Mix the egg and melted/liquid fat together. Add the ground almonds, baking powder and spice if required. Add the fruit if required. Mix well. Put in a small microwaveable pot and microwave on full for three minutes. If you'd prefer not to use a microwave simply cook in the oven for about ten minutes at 180 degrees, and you can even cook lots at a time with a cupcake tray.

For a savoury version, substitute grated carrot or courgette for the fruit, add salt and mixed herbs and some parmesan to the mix instead of the spices. If you make this in a square container it can then be sliced in two to make a sandwich. The muffin travels well and can be used as breakfast on the move or at the office.

INGREDIENTS:

- 50g of Pecans
- 50ml of Water

DIRECTIONS:

Hand blend equal amounts of pecans and water as smoothly as you can. Spoon out into a bowl, and microwave at full whack for 30 seconds. If you'd prefer not to use a microwave simply heat it up on the hob on a medium heat. You've now got a pseudo-porridge to get you ready to rock in the morning. Feel free to add cinnamon, cocoa powder, a handful of blueberries or change it up with other types of nuts or even using milk, coconut milk or almond milk.

INGREDIENTS:

- 1 egg
- 1/4 cup ground almonds or coconut flour (50g)
- Splash of milk/cream
- Knob of butter/coconut oil

DIRECTIONS:

Put the knob of butter in a frying pan on medium heat. Whisk the rest of the ingredients together to make a no-grain-pancake batter and pour into the frying pan once the butter or coconut oil has melted. Fry on one side until just a little batter is left on top, then flip to fry on the other side to make a fully formed flavoursome no-grain-pancake. Add vanilla or cocoa powder for a 'sweeter' pancake and serve with yoghurt and berries. For a savoury version, add herbs, cheese, ham, bacon, tomatoes etc.

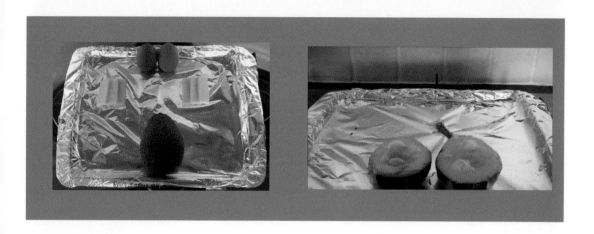

INGREDIENTS:

- 1 Avocado
- 2 Egg Yolks
- 6 Small Slices of Cheese

DIRECTIONS:

Cut the avocado in half and de-stone, place one egg yolk in each half then place the cheese slices around the middle of the avocados. Put in the oven for 10 minutes at 220 degrees and eat to your heart's content.

Although this does make for a great breakfast it just just as easily works as a snack on-the-go or even as part of a lunch box.

INGREDIENTS:

- Bowl of full fat yoghurt
- Nuts/seeds
- Berries

DIRECTIONS:

A trusty mainstay breakfast is full fat yoghurt with nuts/seeds/flax and some berries. You can pot it up the night before for a quick get away to work in the morning. Yoghurt with cocoa or vanilla powder also makes a nice snack or dessert if you need one. There are some lovely flax mixes available now with cocoa or cinnamon flavours. Most health food shops stock them, just be sure to make sure they don't contain SUGAR!

INGREDIENTS:

- Eggs
- Butter/olive oil/coconut oil
- Herbs and spices

DIRECTIONS:

If you have a microwave at work, it is easy to make a big bowl of scrambled eggs for breakfast or lunch. Just break as many eggs as you want (3 is the usual) into a microwaveable bowl and add butter/olive oil/cream/herbs, salt and pepper. Microwave on full for about three minutes, stirring every 30 seconds, until done to your liking. This is another one you can pot up the night before to take to work. You can add chopped ham and tomatoes/spinach and some grated cheese for a more substantial meal.

MAIN MEALS

Here are some ideas for hearty family main meals that are simple to prepare and ea[sy]
to cook. You can add your choice of vegetable accompaniments and tweak them
to suit you and your family. For family members who eat more starchy foods such a[s]
rice and potato you can always put them in bowls in the middle for them to into.

DR JEN'S PASTA FREE LASAGNE – MAIN MEALS

Dr Jen Unwin "We have this quite regularly served with broccoli or green beans. This is a big hit with children. I always make loads hoping for some to be left over to freeze but it hasn't happened yet!"

Follow Dr Jen Unwin on Twitter @jen_unwin

BOLOGNESE INGREDIENTS (4 PORTIONS):

- 500g beef mince
- A large red onion, finely chopped
- Some bacon or chorizo (optional)
- Assorted finely chopped veg (carrot, leek, celery)
- Butter/ghee/coconut oil/olive oil for frying
- Salt, pepper, garlic, herbs, spices, etc.
- Tinned chopped tomatoes or a large jar of passata

BOLOGNESE DIRECTIONS:

Take a large pan and heat the oil. Add the onion and fry for a couple of minutes. Add the bacon/chorizo if you are using it. Fry some more. Add the mince and fry until you get a little browning. Add the tomatoes or passata and herbs etc. Simmer on a low heat for at least 30 mins. Adjust your seasoning to taste.

12/7/23

Dr Jen Unwin "We have this quite regularly served with broccoli or green beans. This is a big hit with children. I always make loads hoping for some to be left over to freeze but it hasn't happened yet!"

Follow Dr Jen Unwin on Twitter @jen_unwin

LASAGNE INGREDIENTS:

- 3 leeks
- Cheddar/parmesan
- Butter/ghee/coconut oil/olive oil

LASAGNE DIRECTIONS:

Slice the leeks to be the same width as your lasagne dish and cut down the middle to the centre of the leek so that when laid flat they make large sheets. Remove the smaller sheets and boil the larger ones for 5 minutes or until tender. Drain the leeks then dry on kitchen roll or tea towels. Using your lasagne dish, pour a thin layer of bolognese into it and then place a layer of leeks along with your favourite cheeses. Repeat a few times, then bake at 220 degrees for about 15 minutes or until the cheese on top is golden brown. Exceedingly delicious with broccoli or green beans.

INGREDIENTS:

- Bolognese from page 12
- 1 large cauliflower
- Butter/ghee/coconut oil/olive oil
- Cheddar

DIRECTIONS:

Whilst the bolognese is cooking, cut the heads of the cauliflower off and boil for about 5 minutes or until soft. Drain the water away and dry with kitchen roll or a tea towel. With a large knob of butter put the cauliflower into a food processor or hand blender and whizz it until it's smooth. Once the bolognese is cooked place it into large oven proof dish and then spread the cauliflower mash over the top and sprinkle as much cheese as you like all over it.

Liver is exceedingly nutritious and also quite cheap. This is a super quick meal and really satisfying, give it a go even if you think you don't like liver.

INGREDIENTS:

- Lamb liver, sliced (enough for the number you are feeding)
- Butter/ghee/coconut oil/olive oil
- Diced onion
- Double cream (small pot for 2-3 people)
- Mustard
- Salt and pepper

DIRECTIONS:

Heat a large frying pan and fry the onion in your favourite oil. Add the sliced liver and stir until nicely browned all over. Put on a lower heat and add the cream, mustard and seasoning. Stir and cook just for a few minutes so it doesn't go rubbery. Serve on fried green cabbage or your favourite green vegetables.

If only having liver is too much for you then alternatively you can always make it half diced beef and half lambs liver!

A scrumptious recipe from one of our founding members, Dr Joanne McCormack. Follow Dr McCormack on Twitter @JoanneReynold14 and visit her website for more recipes and ideas, www.FatIsMyFriend.co.uk

INGREDIENTS:

- 2 slices streaky or other bacon, chopped and sautéed briefly
- 6 eggs beaten
- Handful grated cheddar cheese
- Ghee, butter or coconut oil to grease muffin tin
- Salt and pepper to taste

DIRECTIONS:

Mix all ingredients and pour equal amounts into each muffin hole in a 6 hole muffin tin. Put in an oven at 170 degrees for about 15 minutes, or until the muffins are well risen. Eat with salad and vegetables of your choice.

INGREDIENTS:

- Weekend leftovers
- Butter, salt and pepper

DIRECTIONS:

A real favourite of Dr David Unwin. On a Sunday night he prepares Monday lunch by cooking all the leftovers from the weekend and putting it in a cooking pot along with some butter, salt and pepper. Once it's simmered for a good amount of time mixing all the flavours, he puts it into separate containers to microwave at work. Follow Dr Unwin on Twitter @lowcarbgp

One of our founding members, Dr Trudi Deakin's favourite. This fantastic recipe comes from the X-PERT Health team. Follow them on Twitter @XPERTHealth and be sure to visit their website for some other recipes, www.XpertHealth.org.uk

INGREDIENTS:

- For the crust: 200g ground almonds / 50g coconut oil or butter (melted) / pinch of salt / beaten egg for glazing
- For the filling: 700g stewing diced beef/ 200g diced lamb kidney/ 2 medium diced onions/850ml beef stock

DIRECTIONS:

Make the pastry by melting the coconut oil or butter, add the ground almonds and salt then mix together to form a dough. Refrigerate for about 30 minutes. Heat more butter in a large frying pan, and brown the beef. Set aside, then brown the kidneys on both sides in the same pan. Add the onions and cook for 3-4 minutes. Return the beef to the pan and add the stock, stir well whilst bringing to the boil. Turn the heat down and simmer up to 1½ hours without a lid. Remove from the heat, and add salt and pepper then allow to cool completely. Place the cooked meat mixture into a pie dish. Roll out the pastry (between 2 sheets of cling film) to the pie dish size about 5mm thick. Using a rolling pin, lift the pastry and place it over the top of the pie dish. Trim and crimp the edges with your fingers and thumb. Brush the surface with a beaten egg mixture and bake for 30-40 minutes in a preheated oven at 200 degrees.

Another lovely recipe from one of our founding members, Dr Joanne McCormack. Follow Dr McCormack on Twitter @JoanneReynold14 and visit her website for more recipes and ideas, www.FatIsMyFriend.co.uk

INGREDIENTS (4 PORTIONS):

- For the curry: 4 chicken thighs / 4 drumsticks / 1 cinnamon stick / 5 cardamom pods (crushed lightly in a garlic press) / 4 star anise / 5 cloves / 400ml can coconut milk / 300ml cold water / 1-teaspoon salt
- For the curry paste: 3 tablespoons olive oil or ghee / 300g shallots / 30g root ginger chopped / 5 cloves garlic / 2 tablespoons garam masala / 1 teaspoon ground turmeric / 1 teaspoon hot chilli powder / 1 dessert spoon fish sauce

DIRECTIONS:

Make the curry paste in a food processor by blending all the ingredients until smooth- you may need to stir it a few times in between blending. Dry heat the spices in a large heat proof casserole dish (big enough to take all the chicken) for 2 minutes until you can smell the spices. Add the curry paste and cook for 2-3 minutes, taking care it does not burn. Put the unwashed food processor bowl back on the base and blitz the cauliflower in the bowl so it gets covered in the spicy mixture and becomes the consistency of coarse breadcrumbs. Put them in a wok for later. Add the chicken pieces to the paste, stir, and cook for 5-6 minutes. Keep watching so it does not burn. Add the coconut milk and water and simmer for 15 minutes covered and 30 minutes uncovered. 5 minutes before the chicken is ready blend the heads of a whole cauliflower and heat up in a frying with your favourite oil for the !rice".

INGREDIENTS:

- 1 chicken breast (with skin)
- 1 round lettuce
- 1 tomato
- 1 red pepper
- 1 birdseye chilli
- 1 small red onion
- ½ avocado
- 1 lime
- Butter/ghee/olive oil/oconut oil

DIRECTIONS:

Chop 3/4 of the tomatoes, 1/2 red pepper, birdseye chilli and red onion to make a salsa. Spoon out the avocado and chop up the remaining quarter of the tomato, mix those together, squeeze the lime in and mash it up to make a guacamole. Slice the other 1/2 of the red pepper and chicken into strips, then fry in your favourite oil. Once cooked put on a separate plate. Use the lettuce leaves as tortillas to make the fajitas. With a leaf in hand spread on some salsa, guacamole and place some fried chicken peppers on top. Roll it up and eat it up, but be careful salsa juice is prone to spilling!

Another delicious recipe from Dr Trudi Deakin and the X-PERT Health team. Follow them on Twitter @XPERTHealth and be sure to visit their website for some other recipes, www.XpertHealth.org.uk

INGREDIENTS:

- For the base: 200g shredded mozzarella cheese / 100g grated cheddar cheese / 3 eggs / 1 teaspoon garlic powder / 1 teaspoon dried basil
- For the toppings: 75g pepperoni / 75g salami / 100g mushrooms / 100g pre-fried green peppers / 200g passata / 100g mozzarella cheese

DIRECTIONS:

Mix the cheeses, eggs, garlic powder and basil in well in a mixing bowl. Grease a 16-inch pizza pan or line with greaseproof paper. Evenly spread the cheese mixture in the pan, almost to the edge, making it as thin as possible. Bake at 200 degrees for about 15 minutes or until golden brown.

Once the base is baked spread the passata, toppings and cheese on top. Keeping the oven rack in the centre position, put the pizza under the grill for about 4-5 minutes or until the cheese is melted and bubbly. Remember, variety is the spice of life so be sure to add different toppings each time you make it.

SOUPS & SALADS

Soups are super easy to make and when you cook in bulk they become a very handy on-the-go lunch or for a lazy winter evening meal. Salads are even easier as you can generally make them in under five minutes and usually a lot less. With both soups and salads there is no limit to how creative you can get but here are some ideas for you.

INGREDIENTS:

- Green peppers
- Carrot
- Onion
- Celery
- 1 tbsp tahini
- Grated cheese
- Butter/ghee/olive oil/coconut oil

DIRECTIONS:

Chop equal amounts of green pepper, carrot, onion and celery into soup sized pieces and saute in oil of your choice until softened. I usually start with the pepper and measure from there. Add chilli if you want it really hot, or smoked paprika for more richness, or both and garlic if desired. Add about a litre of a stock of your choice. I use either homemade chicken or vegetable stock. Simmer with the lid on till the veg softens and flavours how you like it. Portion up and stir in tahini stirring till all mixed in. About a tablespoon does the job, but add more if you want it thicker. Stir some good strong grated cheddar in and top with some seeds for crunch, then serve. Remember the tahini will tone down the spiciness a bit and all that stirring in cold stuff will cool the soup, so be sure it's heated up before serving it!

DR JO'S CAULIFLOWER CHEESE SOUP

Another lovely recipe from one of our founding members, Dr Joanne McCormack. Follow Dr McCormack on Twitter @JoanneReynold14 and visit her website for more recipes and ideas, www.FatIsMyFriend.co.uk

INGREDIENTS:

- 1 onion finely chopped
- 900g of cauliflower
- 1 clove garlic crushed
- 1 litre vegetable stock
- 75g cheddar cheese grated
- Whole grain mustard to taste

DIRECTIONS:

Melt some butter and sauté the onion, garlic and cauliflower for a minute, then turn the heat down to low. Stirring it every so often put a lid on the pan and let it cook for 5 minutes. Add the stock, salt and pepper and simmer without a lid for 15 minutes. Add the grated cheese and stir till it has melted, then hand blend to your taste. Finally, add mustard and extra cheese just before serving.

DR JO'S WATERCRESS, LEEK & CREAM SOUP

Dr Joanne McCormack does it again! Follow Dr McCormack on Twitter @JoanneReynold14 and visit her website for more recipes and ideas, www.FatIsMyFriend.co.uk

INGREDIENTS:

- 3 large leeks, chopped roughly
- 2 bunches watercress
- Large knob butter- about 50g
- 850ml chicken or vegetable stock
- 150ml double cream or crème fraiche
- Salt and pepper

DIRECTIONS:

Melt the butter in a saucepan, add the vegetables and stir. Add some salt and let them sweat in the pan with a lid on for 20 minutes. Stir from time to time to stop them sticking. Add the stock and simmer for 15 minutes till tender. Liquidise or sieve the soup to make smooth if wished. Add a dollop of the cream or crème fraiche, & a sprig of watercress when serving.

DR JO'S CREAM OF MUSHROOM SOUP

Another lovely recipe from one of our founding members, Dr Joanne McCormack. Follow Dr McCormack on Twitter @JoanneReynold14 and visit her website for more recipes and ideas, www.FatIsMyFriend.co.uk

INGREDIENTS:

- 300g mushrooms
- 1 onion
- 570ml veggie stock
- Large knob butter
- 200g cream cheese or 150ml single or double cream

DIRECTIONS:

Melt the butter in a saucepan. Add the chopped mushrooms and sweat with the lid on for 15 minutes. Add the stock and cook for another 5-10 minutes. Liquidize and allow to cool. Add the cream cheese and stir till melted.

DR JO'S NECK OF LAMB SOUP

Dr Joanne McCormack does it for the last time! Follow Dr McCormack on Twitter @JoanneReynold14 and visit her website for more recipes and ideas, www.FatIsMyFriend.co.uk

INGREDIENTS:

- 900g neck of lamb
- 1-tablespoon olive oil
- 1 onion
- 2 sticks celery chopped
- 2 clove garlic
- 1 and a half tsp cumin
- 2 teaspoons paprika
- 1 bay leaf
- 1 litre veggie or lamb stock
- 400g chopped tomatoes
- Thick full fat yoghurt to serve

DIRECTIONS:

Sauté the lamb pieces in the oil till browned and set aside. Sauté the vegetables in the spices till softened. Put the meat back in the pan and add the stock. Bring to bubbling point and simmer for 1 hour till tender. Serve with a large dollop of full fat yoghurt.

SAM'S SPINACH, SALMON & STRAWBERRY SALAD

INGREDIENTS:

- 200g of shredded smoked salmon (sugar-free)
- 1 handful of spinach
- 1 handful of spring onions
- 1 handful of yellow bell/capsicum peppers
- 1 handful of strawberries
- 1 shot of olive oil

DIRECTIONS:

We're not sure if putting directions for this is patronising or not, but throw all the ingredients into a bowl and mix until you're satisfied with any added extras that take your fancy, then eat!

INGREDIENTS:

- 115g organic chorizo
- 100g cherry tomatoes
- 1 yellow pepper
- 2 spring onions
- 1 small courgette
- 1 tablespoon of olive oil

DIRECTIONS:

Chop up the vegetables into small-ish chunks then fry them in a non-stick frying pan on medium heat, stirring occasionally. Whilst that is cooking, slice the chorizo sausage and add to the frying pan. Sprinkle some parsley on top and add olive oil to taste. Stir when it's all piping hot, and serve it up!

GREEK SALAD

INGREDIENTS:

- 75g feta cheese
- Handful of olives
- 1 medium cucumber
- 1 large tomato
- 1 small red onion
- Olive oil
- Balsamic vinegar

DIRECTIONS:

Chop up the cucumber, tomato, onion and feta cheese then mix in a large bowl with the olives. Add olive oil, vinegar and some basil over the top to taste. Mix thoroughly again until you have consistently covered the food with oil, vinegar and basil. Either eat straight from the bowl or place on a plate and enjoy.

SNACKS & SIDE DISHE

Super simple standard real food snacks are hard boiled eggs, a handful of nuts
or slices of cheese but here are some ideas for when those don't quite get to the
pit of the problem. Also, here are some side dish ideas that could just as easily be
a snack if you're felling particularly peckish. Remember though, you don't always
need to indulge a snack craving. Sometimes it's a good idea to drink a glass of
water before to see if you're actually hungry or just thirsty.

Another delicious recipe from Dr Trudi Deakin and the X-PERT Health team. Follow them on Twitter @XPERTHealth and be sure to visit their website for some other recipes, www.XpertHealth.org.uk

INGREDIENTS:

- 6 fresh carrots
- 1 tablespoon ground black pepper
- 1 tablespoon red cayenne pepper
- Lard for deep frying
- Salt to taste

DIRECTIONS:

Preheat lard in deep fryer or frying pan to 185 degrees. Cut the carrots into the size of French fries and place in bowl with the pepper. Mix to coat carrots on all sides. Deep fry carrots in batches about 5 minutes until crispy brown and remove carrots to drain. Salt to taste, and omit the pepper if you do not want the carrot fries to be spicy. You could also use peeled swede or celeriac instead of carrots.

INGREDIENTS:

- For the pate: 200g Lamb Liver / 50ml Crème Fraiche or Double Cream / 25g Butter / 1 Small Onion / 1 Clove of Garlic
- For the crackers: 50g of ground almonds / 2 eggs

DIRECTIONS:

Heat the butter in a frying pan, and chop up the liver as finely as you can until the butter is melted. Fry the chopped liver along with any blood for 3 minutes on low heat. Whilst that's frying chop up the small onion and garlic, and then fry it all for a further 3-5 minutes. Leave it all to cool for 5 minutes. Once cooled put all the fried ingredients into a blender, add the 50ml of crème fraiche or double cream and then blend until smooth as pate. For the crackers, crack 2 eggs into a mixing bowl with 50g of ground almonds and whisk until it's thoroughly mixed. Pour the mixture thinly on to a baking tray with buttered greaseproof paper. Bake at 220 degrees for about 10 minutes or until golden brown. If you'd like to dry out your crackers even more you can put them in the microwave for a further minute, which draws out any moisture.

These are so delicious and in expensive to make but people are always impressed. The shop bought ones often have undesirable additives. Ask your butcher for pork rind, with some fat left on, so you can make your own scratchings. Most likely they will slice it for you and I often get mine free if I've bought some other meat at the same time!

INGREDIENTS:

- Pork rind (However much you can fit in your oven)
- Salt (Sea salt or pink Himalayan salt)

DIRECTIONS:

Cut your pork rind into small pieces. Chip-sized scratchings makes for good eating. Then get your oven nice and hot, about 220 degrees. Place the pieces of pork rind in a single layer on a non stick tray or tray lined with non stick foil. Cook for 30-45 minutes until super crisp. Move them about a few times during cooking. Drain the fat off and use for cooking at a later date. Sprinkle with salt, and store in an airtight container on some kitchen roll for a fantastic family snack.

These are nice to make and keep well for a long time. They add a tasty, salt crunch to salads or as a snack with drinks. Julian is a Buddhist and emphasised the importance of making them mindfully, and not multi-tasking or they will burn!

INGREDIENTS:

- A quantity of mixed seeds (pumpkin, sesame, pine nuts, sunflower etc).
- Tamari (wheat free soy)

DIRECTIONS:

Heat up a large non stick frying pan. Dry fry the mixture of seeds over a medium heat, mindfully stirring all the time. Watch out for the seeds browning slightly. Then they are done. Remove from the heat. Tip the seeds into a cold bowl, add 2-3 tablespoons of tamari for each 500g of seeds and mix thoroughly. Return the mixture to the hot pan, this time off the heat and keep stirring, mindfully, until the seeds are dried out. Leave to cool in the pan, and then store in an airtight jar for snacking.

RATATOUILLE - SIDE DISH

Make loads or this as it freezes well and is so useful Also the flavours improve after a few days.

INGREDIENTS:

- A large red onion, finely chopped
- Two red peppers, chopped
- Four medium courgettes, chopped
- A large aubergine, chopped
- Two tins of chopped tomatoes or a jar of passata
- Mixed herbs, salt and pepper
- Olive oil
- Optional: half a glass of red wine, if you have any hanging about.

DIRECTIONS:

In a large pan, heat the oil and fry the onion, add the pepper, keep frying and stirring. Add the courgette and aubergine. Add the tomato and herbs. Transfer to a low heat, put a lid on and simmer gently for about 30 minutes. Take the lid off and keep simmering until you get your required consistency. Adjust the seasoning to taste.

If I have other bits of vegetables hanging around like leeks or celery, I might also use them up, but then it's more of a vegetable stew than a true ratatouille.

INGREDIENTS:

- 1 courgette
- Olives, sliced
- Olive oil
- Cheese of choice (Cheddar or mozzarella work well)

DIRECTIONS:

Slice the courgette in half, base with olive oil and bake in a pre-heated oven at 200 degrees for 10 minutes. Once soft in the middle sprinkle sliced olives over the courgette-halves and then place your cheese of choice on top and bake for a further 2-3 minutes until the cheese turns a golden brown. Feel free to add some cherry tomatoes whilst baking the courgette-halves to add some extra flavour.

INGREDIENTS:

- Cauliflower (As much as you like)
- Cheese of choice (Cheddar or mozzarella work well)

DIRECTIONS:

Cut off the cauliflower florets and boil in a pan for about 5 minutes. Drain the water once slightly soft and place into a deep oven dish. Cover the cauliflower with either regular cheese if you're in a rush or use the cheese sauce from the sauce section in this book. Then bake everything for about 30 minutes at 200 degrees. Sprinkling some pine nuts and parsley on the cauliflower before the cheese gives is great if you fancy being adventurous!

INGREDIENTS:

- A large celeriac, peeled and sliced thinly
- 300ml cream
- Chopped garlic
- Salt and pepper

DIRECTIONS:

Take a butter greased oven proof dish and layer celeriac, cream and a sprinkle of garlic, salt and pepper and repeat. Cover the dish with foil and bake at 200 degrees for 45-60 mins. Test by poking it with a knife in the middle to see if the celeriac is cooked. You can add grated cheese and/or butter to your layers if you want to make it richer and creamer.

VEGETABLE SIDE CURRY - SIDE DISH

INGREDIENTS:

- Red onion, finely diced
- Mushrooms, finely chopped
- A cauliflower, chopped and diced
- Curry spice mix, your choosing
- Coconut oil for frying
- Salt and pepper

DIRECTIONS:

Take a large frying pan, heat the oil and fry the onion. Add the spice mix and heat though. Add the mushrooms and fry. Add the cauliflower and then move to a lower heat and keep stirring until it is cooked through. I like it when it still is a bit "al dente".

SAUCES

Often when strapped for time a meal can be as simple as a steak, some vegetable and sauce poured on top. Here are some ideas for sauces to help mix things up for th times as well as accompaniments for other meals when you have more time.

CHEESE SAUCE

Use this as a sauce on vegetables, meat, fish and dishes such as lasagne. It is practically instant and makes anything very tasty!

INGREDIENTS:

- 200ml double cream
- Cheese of choice grated or small cubes (mature cheddar or stilton work very well)
- 1 tsp mustard
- Salt and pepper to taste

DIRECTIONS:

Gently heat the cream for a few minutes, then add the cheese, mustard and seasoning and stir until fully melted in and a smooth sauce forms. Use any extra seasoning you like to spice it up!

PESTO - SAUCE

A definite taste of the Mediterranean. Delicious on lamb or beef steaks and drizzled over vegetables or salads.

INGREDIENTS:

- 400ml Olive oil
- Large bunch of basil
- 50g pine nuts
- 25g grated parmesan
- 2 garlic cloves
- Salt to taste

DIRECTIONS:

Hand blend all the ingredients until smooth. It's worth noting that some like it super-smooth and others prefer it a bit crunchy, so it's worth experimenting to find out how you prefer it. Also, all the amounts can be varied to taste, so less cheese and nuts and more oil will make a 'thinner' pesto and visa versa. We love the garlic but some in our family prefer it without. If you have any leftover keep it in a jar in a fridge.

HAZEL'S YOGHURT SAUCE

My mum used to make this in the summer and serve it with salmon and green beans or peas. It is marked 'v.v.g.' in her hand written recipe book, which was the highest accolade (very, very, good!) It was my daughter's favourite meal for a while too. It goes really well with any fish and is again, super speedy to prepare.

INGREDIENTS:

- Small bunches of herbs (parsley, mint, chives and dill)
- 500ml full fat yoghurt
- 100ml olive oil
- Juice of half a lemon
- Salt and pepper to taste

DIRECTIONS:

Hand blend all the ingredients until smooth and adjust the seasoning to taste.

INGREDIENTS:

- 2 large egg yolk
- 2 tbsp fresh lemon juice
- 2 tbsp water
- 1 tsp dry mustard
- 1 tsp salt
- 2 cup of olive oil

DIRECTIONS:

Heat the egg yolks, lemon juice and water in a small frying pan over very low heat, stirring constantly. At the first sign of thickness, remove from heat and submerge in a large pan of cold water (you should continue stirring here to avoid creating citrus-y scrambled eggs...trust us!) Scoop the mixture out of the pan and into a food processor. Blend for a few seconds and then let the mixture sit uncovered for at least 5 minutes to cool. Add the mustard and salt to taste, and blend on low speed. Drizzle the olive oil slowly into the mixture whilst stirring until all ingredients are combined. Scoop into a large glass container and chill immediately. Mayonnaise should keep for at least one week if stored correctly.

FRENCH DRESSING - SAUCE

Some prefer this to mayonnaise on a salad as you can get a good coating rather than blobs!

INGREDIENTS:

- 200ml olive oil
- 100ml balsamic vinegar
- 1 tsp mustard
- Salt and pepper
- Optional: ginger, garlic, chilli, mixed herbs, etc.

DIRECTIONS:

Put the ingredients in a jar or other lidded pot, and with your hand on top shake like there's no tomorrow! As always adjust with the any seasoning you like.

TREATS

After years of a real food lifestyle your sweet tooth certainly reduces but that doesn't mean you can't treat yourself or your family! These recipes aren't for everyday eating but are occasional treats for parties and special occasions.

Sometimes it has to be done. I've adapted this from other things I've tried and it seems reliable. Also you can alter the flavourings according to your mood and taste.

Follow Dr Jen Unwin on Twitter @jen_unwin

INGREDIENTS (For a loaf tin sized cake tin):

- 5 eggs
- 2 Tbsp coconut oil
- Vanilla powder or mixed spice
- 1/2 tsp baking powder
- 1 banana
- 2 tbsp each of coconut & almond flour
- 2 tbsp ground flax

DIRECTIONS:

Blend up the eggs, oil and banana. Add the dry ingredients and stir gently. Should be a "cake mix" consistency. If too runny add more almond flour. At this stage you can add any extra things you want (we have tried, blueberries, chopped pecans, 85% dark chocolate fragments etc). Pour the mixture into a lined loaf tin and bake on a medium heat for about 30 minutes. Can be served with cream or yoghurt. For a celebration cake, make the ganache on the next page and ice your cake with that!

The ultimate treat! Ganache can be served with berries or as an icing on a cake.

Follow Dr Jen Unwin on Twitter @jen_unwin

INGREDIENTS:

- 200g dark chocolate (more than 70%-we are unto 90% now and it works with that)
- 600ml double cream

DIRECTIONS:

Break the chocolate bar into small piece and place in a bowl. Gently heat the cream in a pan and when just coming to a simmer pour it over the chocolate and keep stirring until the chocolate melts. Keep stirring and as it cools it will thicken. YUMMY YUMMY, GET IN MY TUMMY!

FRIDGE TIFFIN - TREAT

Quick to make and keeps well in the fridge!

INGREDIENTS:

- 3 tbsp coconut oil
- Vanilla powder
- 200g dark chocolate (at least 70%)
- Desiccated coconut (optional)
- Seed mix (optional)
- 100% peanut butter (optional)
- Ground almonds

DIRECTIONS:

Melt the coconut oil and dark chocolate. Add the 100% peanut butter if you are using it or if you prefer any other nut butter, use that instead. Then add the dried coconut, seeds and enough almond flour to make a stiffish mixture.

Press into a small tray or container lined with cling film. Chill overnight or until set, then chop into pieces and return to the fridge until it's time to eat.

LUCY LU'S ICE POPS - TREAT

Great for little children on a sunny day! I use disposal wine glasses and plastic cocktail stirrers to make them look special.

INGREDIENTS:

- Coconut water or coconut milk
- Mixed berries
- Grapes

DIRECTIONS:

Push one end of your cocktail stirrer into a grape and place the grape in the bottom of the glass. Add chopped fruit around the stick to hold it upright. carefully poor the coconut water or milk on the fruit until covered. Freeze and have a cool summer's day!

INGREDIENTS:

- 75g of chia seeds
- 200ml of unsweetened almond milk
- 4 almond milk ice cubes
- 1 tbsp of 100% cocoa powder
- 1 tbsp of desiccated coconut

DIRECTIONS:

Put all the ingredients into a high speed blender and blend for 30 seconds. Either eat straight from the blender or put it in the fridge for 30 minutes to help it set and have a gooier texture.

INGREDIENTS:

- 100g strawberry
- 100g full fat yoghurt

DIRECTIONS:

Put both the strawberries and yoghurt in a high speed blender until smooth. Pour the mixture into an ice cube tray and place lollipop sticks or cocktail sticks in each cube diagonally. Place the tray in a freezer overnight or for a few hours. Before trying to take them out individually cut across the cube grid of the tray with a knife and then you can enjoy!

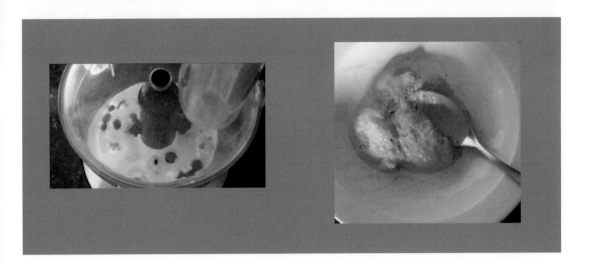

INGREDIENTS:

- 100g frozen blueberries
- 100ml single cream
- 2 tsp 100% cocoa powder

DIRECTIONS:

Put the frozen blueberries in a food processor followed by the cocoa powder. Then pour the cream over the top until the blueberries are just covered. Wait for at least 2 minutes whilst the cream freezes. Some creams might take more like 4 minutes to freeze. Once the cream freezes, turn on the food processor for 30 seconds, and you're ice cream is made. Use a spoon to scoop into a bowl with 2 or 3 scoops per person, and add any extras such as nuts, cinnamon or dark chocolate.

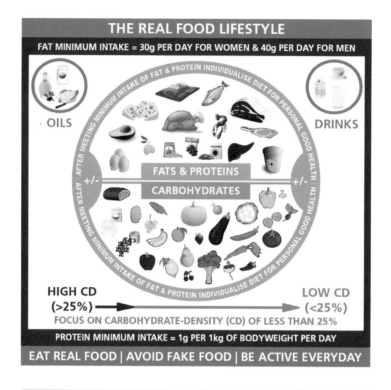

THE REAL FOOD LIFESTYLE

FAT MINIMUM INTAKE = 30g PER DAY FOR WOMEN & 40g PER DAY FOR MEN

AFTER MEETING MINIMUM INTAKE OF FAT & PROTEIN INDIVIDUALISE DIET FOR PERSONAL GOOD HEALTH

OILS

DRINKS

+/-   FATS & PROTEINS   +/-
CARBOHYDRATES

AFTER MEETING MINIMUM INTAKE OF FAT & PROTEIN INDIVIDUALISE DIET FOR PERSONAL GOOD HEALTH

HIGH CD (>25%) ➜ LOW CD (<25%)

FOCUS ON CARBOHYDRATE-DENSITY (CD) OF LESS THAN 25%

PROTEIN MINIMUM INTAKE = 1g PER 1kg OF BODYWEIGHT PER DAY

EAT REAL FOOD | AVOID FAKE FOOD | BE ACTIVE EVERYDAY

THE REAL FOOD LIFESTYLE FOR WEIGHT LOSS

CREATE A PERSONAL PURPOSE AS TO WHY YOU WANT TO LOSE WEIGHT...

EAT FATS & PROTEINS UNTIL HUNGER IS SATISFIED AND AVOID CONSTANT SNACKING

OILS

DRINKS

FATS & PROTEINS
NON-STARCHY CARBOHYDRATES

BE ACTIVE EVERYDAY

NUTS & SEEDS (<100G A DAY)

REDUCE TOTAL CARBOHYDRATE TO <130G PER DAY FOCUSING ON NON STARCHY CARBOHYDRATES

...BECAUSE WITH A STRONG ENOUGH WHY YOU CAN OVERCOME ANY HOW

EAT REAL FOOD | AVOID FAKE FOOD | BE ACTIVE EVERYDAY

DOWNLOAD FREE REAL FOOD BOOKLETS OR BUY PRINTED SAMPLE PACKS @ www.PHCuk.org/Booklets

A BIG THANK YOU TO ALL THAT HELPED WITH REAL FOOD ROCKS!

Printed in Poland
by Amazon Fulfillment
Poland Sp. z o.o., Wrocław